Fit for Mission?

Marriage

Preparation Course

Couple's Book

Patrick O'Donoghue - Bishop of Lancaster

With the collaboration of the Diocese of Lancaster's
Marriage and Family Life Commission

CATHOLIC TRUTH SOCIETY
Publishers to the Holy See

Message to Couples

What is the best thing to say to a young couple beginning this marriage preparation course? All kinds of ideas and advice spring to mind, but I think the best thing I can do is tell you a story:

This story is about Marilyn Monroe and her marriage to Arthur Miller, the American writer. As you may know, though Marilyn was a beautiful and famous movie star, she struggled her whole life with low self-esteem and addiction. Arthur Miller recounts standing over Marilyn, watching her sleeping, 'I found myself straining to imagine miracles. What if she were to wake and I were able to say, 'God loves you, darling,' and she were able to believe it! How I wish I still had my religion and she hers'.

Marilyn Monroe and Arthur Miller weren't Catholics, but this story sums up for me what a good Catholic marriage is all about.

Being a husband and wife means always wanting the best for each other, wanting each other to be happy and fulfilled, wanting each other to feel safe and wanted, wanting each other to feel appreciated and attractive, wanting each other to feel important and needed.

I don't know how religious you both are, or even if you still go to Mass or pray, but I do know that by wanting to get married in a Catholic church you want religion to play some part in the most important day of your lives together, your wedding.

You might not have realised this when you chose to have a Catholic wedding, but –whether you believe in God or not or in his Son Jesus Christ – when you make your marriage vows to each other on the day, God becomes part of your lives and your relationship in a very special way. You'll find out more about this during the course.

During your married life together, you're going to have very good times together, because you love each other, and you're going to have tough times together, because you love each other. During the tough times I want you to remember what Arthur Miller wanted Marilyn Monroe to believe, 'God loves you, darling'. This will help you both. And also remember, the Church is here to help you in the tough times and celebrate with you in the good times: you only have to ask.

✠ *Patrick O'Donoghue*
Bishop of Lancaster.

Overview

AIM OF THE PROGRAMME

To prepare you to receive the Sacrament of Marriage

SESSION 1

Two become one

SESSION 2

Love is...?

SESSION 3

Respect the differences

SESSION 4

God's body talk

SESSION 5

Jesus' helping hand

SESSION 6

Loving each other in Christ

Welcome to the Marriage Preparation Course

This overview is designed to introduce you to what you can expect over the next few weeks.

There are 6 sessions in the programme, as shown in the panel down the side. For each session you have a Session Summary for Couples.

The Session Summary gives:

- the aims and objectives for each session;
- the key features of the session to act as a memory jogger of what the session covered, and
- other material relevant to the session.

The sessions all contain some formal input time and some discussion time and activities. The Presenters will share some of their own experiences with you and you may like to share ideas with the group but you will not have to do anything you are uncomfortable with. Discussions are confidential to the group.

If there are any areas covered on the course that you would like to know more about the Presenters can help with your questions and give you a Reading List or source of material for the topics. Scripture references are from the Revised Standard Version (Catholic Edition).

We hope that you enjoy the course.

Session 1
Two become one

AIM

To introduce the course and make connections between your experience of love and the Church's teaching on love

OBJECTIVES

By the end of this session, you will be able to:

- Describe the connection between your love and the God of love
- Explain God's meaning and purpose for marriage
- Discuss the opportunities and challenges of marriage
- Start to plan how to deepen your love for each other

PRAYER - OUR FATHER

Our Father who art in heaven, hallowed be thy name. Thy kingdom come, thy will be done on earth as it is in Heaven. Give us this day our daily bread and forgive us our trespasses as we forgive those who trespass against us. And lead us not into temptation but deliver us from evil. Amen.

Since God created man and woman, their mutual love becomes an image of the absolute and unfailing love with which God loves man. It is good, very good, in the Creator's eyes. And this love which God blesses is intended to be fruitful and to be realised in the common work of watching over creation: "And God blessed them and God said to them: 'Be fruitful and multiply, and fill the earth and subdue it.'"

(*Catechism of the Catholic Church*, CCC 1604)

Activity: Getting to know each other

We're all here because we know love is important, maybe the most important thing in our lives. Talk about the following questions in your couples for a few minutes (say, 5 minutes), then we'll come together to share.

1. Where did you first meet?
2. When did you know you were in love?
3. What does being in love feel like?
4. How have you changed each other's lives?
5. How do you know the other person loves you?

Your love as baptised Christians in all its aspects – emotional, sexual and spiritual – is a special participation in God's love

Activity: What's God got to do with our marriage?

Through the Bible, God shows us what he's like, who he is and what he's interested in. Over the 3,800 years we've known him, God has made it very clear that he's interested in marriage, and how husbands and wives love each other and their children. The passages in this session help show why we believe that 'God is love'. The passion, commitment and joy you find in loving each other gives you a special understanding, (though a limited one!), of God's love for each one of us. Don't worry - the Bible is very relevant to love.

As a couple, discuss the question 'What strikes you about this passage?' for the passage(s) you have been allocated (take about 5 minutes). We'll then come together to share.

What strikes you about this passage?

(A) The LORD says: Sing for joy O heavens, and exult O earth; break forth O mountains into singing! For the Lord has comforted his people [Israel], and will have compassion on his suffering ones. But Israel said, "The Lord has forsaken me, my Lord has forgotten me". Can a woman forget her baby at the breast; feel no pity for the child she has borne? Even if these were to forget, I shall not forget you. Look, I have engraved you on the palms of my hands.

(Isaiah 49:13-16)

(B) The LORD says: Therefore, I will now attract her [Israel], and bring her into the wilderness, and speak tenderly to her... On that day, says the Lord, you will call me, "My husband"... And I will take you for my wife forever; I will take you for my wife in righteousness and in justice, in steadfast love, and in mercy. I will take you for my wife in faithfulness; and you shall know the Lord.

(Hosea 2:14-20)

(C) The LORD says: I have loved you [Israel] with an everlasting love; therefore I have continued my faithfulness to you. Again I will build you, and you shall be built, O virgin Israel! Again you shall take your tambourines, and go forth in the dance of the merrymakers... Then shall the young women rejoice in the dance, and the young men and the old shall be merry. I will turn their mourning into joy; I will comfort them, and give them gladness for sorrow.

(Jeremiah 31:3, 13)

(D) The LORD says: You [Israel] grew up and became tall and arrived at full womanhood; your breasts were formed, and your hair had grown; yet you were naked and bare. I passed by you again and looked on you; you were at the age for love. I spread the edge of my cloak over you and covered your nakedness: I pledged myself to you and entered into a covenant [marriage] with you, says the Lord God, and you became mine... I clothed you with embroidered cloth and with sandals of fine leather; I bound you in fine linen and covered you with rich fabric...You grew exceedingly beautiful, fit to be a queen.

(Ezekiel 16:7-13)

Activity: What is marriage?

As a couple, read the statements below and decide whether or not you agree with them and why (take about 10 minutes).

We will then discuss the questions as a group.

Statement	Strongly Disagree	Disagree	Depends	Agree	Strongly Agree
1. Marriage should be about total mutual self-giving – this is best expressed through sexual love.				✓	
2. If a couple is having a rough time with each other it is better for them, and for their children, to get divorced.	✓				
3. If no one finds out, having sex with someone else occasionally can add spice to life without spoiling the marriage.	✓				
4. It is OK to get married and agree never to have children.				✓	

God loves Israel with a passion! He expresses his love in terms of total commitment, he will be totally faithful, and expects Israel to be totally faithful in return and belong to him. His love is expressed in very physical terms; he is concerned with the material well-being of his people. God wants us to have fun and to enjoy life. Throughout the Bible the image of the wedding is used to convey the happiness and fulfilment that God wants for the whole human race.

God isn't afraid to express his love for humanity in erotic terms. The Bible is clear that sexual attraction and feelings are good, and an important part of love between a husband and wife. Sex in itself is good, though - as you know - sometimes what people do with sex can be immoral and harmful.

There are four essential qualities of Christian marriage

1. **Personal unity.** Sexual love is essential for the wellbeing of the marriage. Sex isn't just a biological act, but involves the innermost being of each person. Through sexual love husband and wife 'speak' the language of total self-gift, through which they give themselves to each other physically, psychologically, personally and spiritually. Total giving is for life without conditions.

2. **Indissolubility.** When a man and woman give consent during the marriage ceremony to mutually give themselves to each other they form a bond that is sealed by God himself. When the words of self-giving are consummated by the sexual act of self-giving, the marriage can never be dissolved. The husband and wife enjoy a bond that can be described as forming 'one heart and soul'. Therefore marriage is indissoluble and so forbids divorce.

3. **Faithfulness or fidelity.** When you give yourself in sexual love totally to your husband or wife and accept the gift of the other, there is a body language of total trust, total commitment and a promise of faithfulness. By its nature, sexual love requires that it is exclusive to marriage. The anger, sense of betrayal and despair that occurs when a husband or wife discover their partner has committed adultery is a true measure of the importance of faithfulness in sexual love. Adultery makes a lie of all the words and acts of love, and is experienced as the most hurtful and destructive rejection. The sexual act is never a purely biological act, it is always personal and deeply affects the person.

4. **Openness to fertility.** If a couple get married but have no intention of having children there is no marriage. The intention to have children is so important to the meaning and purpose of marriage that to totally reject having children means there is no marriage. The basic purpose of sexual love is the procreation of children, and the creation of a loving and stable family for their wellbeing and education. If a couple intend to have children, but due to infertility cannot conceive children, the intention is enough to make the marriage as real and true as one that has children.

Lord God, the source of all love, your loving plan has brought us together. As we prepare for the sacrament of marriage, strengthen our hearts, so that we will keep faith with each other, please you in all things, and so come to the happiness of our wedding day.

Amen.

Session 2
Love is...?

AIM

To deepen your understanding of love and how to increase your love

OBJECTIVES

By the end of this session, you will be able to:

- State the Christian understanding of love
- Discuss the opportunities and challenges of marriage
- Accept the benefits to marriage of leading a virtuous life
- Describe how the deadly sins endanger marriage
- Apply practical strategies for leading a virtuous life

Activity: How will being married be different?

Being married will bring about differences in your life. Here are some things which others have said about the difference marriage makes. Take time together as a couple to think about which apply to you (say 10 minutes). Are there any you would like to discuss further? Are there any differences you would add?

- It is great to share everything: our house, our daily lives, ourselves...
- It is wonderful to have that commitment both ways! Till death do us part.
- It's great not having to live with the anxiety that the other might decide it's not working anymore and leave.
- It's a relief to be able to share everything about myself with someone I completely trust.
- It provides the right environment for bringing up our children.
- Other people think of us and treat us differently as a married couple.
- The grace that God gives through marriage helps us to stay together through the difficult times.
- It is the best possible way to express our love for each other.
- Having the blessing of the Church and all our friends and family on our love is very powerful.

Activity: What is love?

Together as a couple, consider the following examples of love. Then answer this question: Which description(s) best describe love and why do you think so? (Take 10 minutes).

1. Mary was very fond of John. She liked the way he laughed so much at silly things, that the tears ran down his face and the way he wiggled his feet in the air and rolled around the settee. For days afterwards it brought a smile to her face remembering his uncontrolled laughing.
2. Bill really enjoyed playing tennis with Julia, because she was competitive and was helping him improve his service. Best of all, Bill enjoyed going to the pub afterwards with Julia and just talking about things.
3. Let him kiss me with the kisses of his mouth, for your love-making is sweeter than wine; delicate is the fragrance of your perfume, your name is an oil poured out.
4. Alice thought Tom very brave but worried that after the operation he would never be well again. The doctors said he could live a normal life with one kidney; there was a million-to-one chance that he was a match for a kidney transplant to his brother, but still… Tom said he had to give his brother a chance to live, even if they hadn't got on for years.

The Greeks had four words for four different types of love – affection (*storge*), friendship (*philia*), erotic love (*eros*) and self-giving love (*agape*).

Affection cherishes and appreciates the uniqueness of the other, makes allowances for the irritating things they do and makes the other feel safe and wanted.

Friendship is a non-sexual type of love, sharing and caring for someone on a deeply personal level.

Erotic love including the sexual act, is meaningful on a personal level; it makes both feel valued, appreciated, respected and recognized as a person.

Self-giving love sacrifices your own needs or happiness for the needs and happiness of the other.

"If I speak in the tongues of men and of angels, but have not love, I am a noisy gong or a clanging cymbal. And if I have prophetic powers, and understand all mysteries and all knowledge, and if I have all faith, so as to remove mountains, but have not love, I am nothing. If I give away all I have, and if I deliver my body to be burned, but have not love, I gain nothing. Love is patient and kind; love is not jealous or boastful; it is not arrogant or rude. Love does not insist on its own way; it is not irritable or resentful; it does not rejoice at wrong, but rejoices in the right. Love bears all things, believes all things, hopes all things, endures all things. Love never ends; as for prophecies, they will pass away; as for tongues, they will cease; as for knowledge, it will pass away... So faith, hope, love abide, these three; but the greatest of these is love."

(1 Corinthians 13:1-8,13)

"For God so loved the world that he gave his only Son, so that everyone who believes in him may not perish but may have eternal life."

(John 3:16)

Activity: The fruits of love

Love changes the way that we act. If we are filled with love then the way we behave will change. The secrets to a happy marriage are those behaviours which come from love. These are: charity, joy, peace, patience, kindness, goodness, faithfulness, modesty, self-control, chastity, generousity and gentleness. The threats to a happy marriage are those behaviours which do not come from love such as pride, avarice, lust, wrath, gluttony, envy, and sloth.

For this activity look at the descriptions below and match them to the virtue or vice listed. If you have time, you could start thinking about which virtues are the most important to you as a couple and which vices are the worst (about 15 minutes). Afterwards we'll come together to discuss.

Virtues/Fruits of the Holy Spirit: charity, joy, peace, patience, kindness, goodness, faithfulness, modesty, self-control, chastity, generousity and gentleness.

	Virtue	Description	Ranking of importance
goodness	SELF CONTROL	To act in a way you know deep down is the right thing to do.	
✓	PEACE	A state of calmness and relaxation, where there is emotional balance and harmony.	
joy	chastity	The focus of your sexual desire on, and activity with, your spouse. In marriage it is the complete and lifelong mutual gift of a man and a woman.	
self giving	KINDNESS	Ultimately sacrifice; it is the willingness to lay down one's life for another.	
✓	GENEROSITY	An open and forgiving largeness of soul that is prepared to give.	3
patience	GENTLENESS	To receive or suffer unwelcome actions whatever the source with calmness and resolve to endure come what may.	4
self cont	MODESTY	Personal integrity and involves the practice of saying 'no' to one's self.	
gentleness	PATIENCE	Not weakness but quiet self possession, control of self and responding without self-assertion and violence.	
Joy	FAITHFULNESS	Not to be confused with pleasure or happiness, rather it is an inner sense that you are in the right place, doing the right thing, with the person you want to be with for the rest of your life, as God intends.	1
faith	GOODNESS	Keeping promises and commitments, being dependable, reliable.	5
kind	GENTLENESS	Respectful and tender care for the needs of the other.	2
modesty	KINDNESS	Purity of heart that protects the intimate privacy of the person with patience, decency and discretion.	

Vices: pride, avarice, lust, wrath, gluttony, envy, and sloth. Match the descriptions below to these vices, and rank by order of the seriousness of the threat each vice poses to marriage.

Vice	Description	Ranking
✓ Gluttony	Excessive consumption, or immoderation or an inordinate desire for food.	4
✓ WRATH	A desire for revenge, a deliberate desire to kill or seriously wound a neighbour.	1
✓ PRIDE	The feeling that you are better than everyone else.	2
✓ Sloth	Not only laziness but a refusal to do what you know is the right thing to do because you just can't be bothered.	3
✓ AVARICE	Arises from a passion for riches and the power, status and celebrity that comes with being rich.	7
✓ ENVY	Refers to the sadness at the sight of another's goods and the immoderate desire to acquire them for oneself, even unjustly.	5
✓ LUST	The disorder of sexual desire, when you want to pleasure yourself on another as if they were a plaything and not a person. This happens in marriage when you use each other for sexual pleasure, with no expression of love or openness to fertility.	6

Action Planning

As a couple consider what you will do differently as a result of this session.

STOP: Is there anything you should **stop** doing?

START: What will you **start** doing?

CONTINUE: What are the things you should **continue** doing – or do even more of?

Session 3 Respect the differences

AIM

To establish practical ways of positively engaging with the differences between man and woman and explore how these can be the source of marriage's strength and richness, but also a source of misunderstanding, conflict and hurt

OBJECTIVES

By the end of this session, you will be able to:

- Explain that God made males and females to complement and complete each other
- Use effective strategies for speaking and listening
- Indicate ways of resolving conflicts
- Accept the importance of forgiveness and what this means

"Put on then compassion, kindness, lowliness, meekness and patience, forbearing one another and, if one has a complaint against another, forgiving each other; as the Lord has forgiven you, so you also must forgive. And above all these put on love, which binds everything together in perfect harmony."

(Colossians 3:12-14)

Activity: Respect the differences

Sometimes you may hear talk about men and women as if they were two different species. However, the differences between masculinity and femininity have their origin in God's will and purpose for men and women.

Take time now together as a couple to think about what ways you are different from, or the same as, each other. (Take about 10-12 minutes).

- The things you like doing… What do you like to do to relax and recharge? What energises you?
- How do you like to receive information? (e.g. general outline vs. great detail).
- The ways you react to things… What guides you most when you react and/or make decisions? (e.g. objective logic vs. values and feelings).
- The way you do things… Do you prefer order or flexibility? (e.g. carefully scheduled plans vs. flexible spontaneity).

Strategies for listening effectively (PEARS)

- **Probe:** Use open questions to really understand what the speaker is saying; that is, use questions which demand a fuller answer than "yes" or "no" to encourage the other person to explain more fully: e.g. "tell me a bit more about that".
- **Empathise:** Respect and reflect the underlying feelings, put yourself in the speaker's position.
- **Awareness:** Be aware of our tendency to distort and really seek to understand what the other person is trying to say; build on the speaker's ideas; do not change direction or take control of the discussion.
- **Respond non-verbally:** Show attention, make good eye contact, respond naturally.
- **Summarise:** Use your own words to paraphrase what you think you've heard to check you've got it right and show that you have really been listening; do not just repeat the speaker verbatim.

Strategies for effective speaking

- **Love:** Remind yourself that you love your spouse and that he or she loves you.
- **Intention:** Think what you are trying to say before you start to speak.
- **Attention:** Tell your spouse what you need of them (e.g. "I just need you to listen to me for a minute, as there's something I want to tell you").
- **Clarity:** Use short sentences.
- **Unity:** Avoid the language of blame. Talk instead about what you would like to be different, (e.g. instead of: "it's your fault the kids were left at school - you never remember when it's your turn to pick them up!" you could say: "I would like us to agree a way of making sure you remember when it's your turn to pick the kids up from school.").
- **Expression:** As well as thinking about what you are going to say, it is important to remember that messages are a complex mix of what can be called words, music and dance.
    - The words are what you say;
    - The music is your tone of voice and expression;
    - The dance is all the body language you use to express yourself: eye contact, facial expression, gesture.

Activity: Speaking and listening effectively

- Think of an event in your own lives that you could use to practise 'speaking and listening'. Perhaps a happy event, e.g. an outing you have enjoyed together.
- Decide who is going to start as the Speaker and who will start as the Listener.
- Give the Speaker the couple's book to hold. He / she has the 'floor' whilst holding it.
- As the Speaker you break down what you want to say into clear points to ensure that all you want to say is actually said.
- As the Listener you want to try to be an effective listener (remember Pears). In particular, summarise or paraphrase what the Speaker has said to show that you have heard and clearly understood the message. It is important that you concentrate on what the Speaker is saying and don't respond with explanations of your own, or retaliations.
- When the Speaker has finished and is happy that the Listener has understood, the Speaker and Listener should change roles and work through the steps again with the new Speaker presenting his or her side of the events, feelings etc.

(You have about 10 minutes for the activity; try to share the time equally between you so you each have 5 minutes when you are Speaker and 5 minutes when you are Listener).

A useful tool to help you talk openly and constructively about behaviours or situations that upset or threaten you is 'EEC'. This stands for Example, Effect, Change or Continue.

Example of using EEC:

- **E** xample: When you contradicted me in front of our friends last night.
- **E** ffect: I felt embarrassed and angry.
- **C** hange: I don't want you to contradict me in public; can you tell me about your different point of view when we get home?

Activity: What do we do when we are faced with conflict?

- Working in pairs, take a couple of minutes to think of one or two occasions recently when you disagreed or argued with each other. (Say 2 mins).
- Individually, jot down how you acted or use the tick boxes below. Tick as many boxes as are relevant, (e.g., did you shout, become sarcastic, make a joke of it etc.). Then jot down how your boyfriend / girlfriend acted. (Say 5 mins).
- Finally compare notes and consider: "What aspects of your boyfriend's / girlfriend's way of handling the disagreement did you find helpful and which unhelpful?" (say 8 mins).

ME	YOU
❑ Become sarcastic	❑ Become sarcastic
❑ Become angry and shout	❑ Become angry and shout
❑ Become defensive	❑ Become defensive
❑ Become quiet and withdrawn	❑ Become quiet and withdrawn
❑ Ignore the whole issue	❑ Ignore the whole issue
❑ Make a joke of it	❑ Make a joke of it
❑ Try to calm the situation	❑ Try to calm the situation
❑ Try to listen	❑ Try to listen
❑ Talked about it	❑ Talked about it
❑ Other (please describe)	❑ Other (please describe)

Action Planning

As a couple consider what you will do differently as a result of this session. You might like to consider the following:

- How will you make sure you listen effectively to one another?
- How will you make sure how you speak to one another shows love and respect?
- How will you resolve conflicts that arise between you?

PRAYER

I confess to Almighty God that I have sinned through my own fault, in my thoughts and in my words, in what I have done, and in what I have failed to do and I ask the blessed Mary, ever virgin, all the angels and saints, to pray for me to the Lord our God.

Session 4
God's body Talk

AIM

To appreciate that being created by the God of love our bodies reflect their origin in his loving purpose. This purpose informs what is the right and wrong use of our bodies

OBJECTIVES

By the end of this session, you will be able to:

- Explain the meaning and purpose God has given sexual love
- State why contraception and IVF contradict the meaning of marital love
- State why the marriage vows of unity, indissolubility, faithfulness and openness to life are vital to the success of a marriage
- Explain why the Church advocates natural fertility awareness

"The human person: with our openness to truth and beauty, our sense of moral goodness, our freedom and the voice of our conscience, with our longings for the infinite and for happiness, we question ourselves about God's existence. In all this we discern signs of our spiritual soul. The soul, the "seed of eternity we bear in ourselves, irreducible to the merely material" can have its origin only in God."

(*CCC* 33)

Sing for joy, O heavens, and exult, O earth; break forth, O mountains, into singing! For the Lord has comforted his people, and will have compassion on his suffering ones. Can a woman forget her nursing child, or show no compassion for the child of her womb? Even these may forget, yet I will not forget you. See, I have inscribed you on the palms of my hands; your cries are continually before me.

(Isaiah 49:13, 15-16)

Made in the image of God

Read the statements below and decide as a couple whether or not you agree with them and why. (Take about 10 minutes). We will then discuss the questions as a group.

Statement	Strongly Disagree	Disagree	Depends	Agree	Strongly Agree
Humans are just like the other animals, nothing more.	✓				
The order and beauty of the world and the universe show us everything has been created by God.					
Sex is primarily for pleasure.					
People can do selfless things for love of others.					

Why contraception and IVF are wrong? True or false

Read the statements below and decide as a couple whether they are true or false, giving reasons. (Take about 5 minutes).[1]

We will then discuss the questions as a group.

Statement	True	False
1. The Church is against contraception because sex is something bad and dirty.		X
2. The Church is against contraception because it wants every act of sexual love to result in a baby.		X
3. The Church is against contraception because it makes a lie out of God's language of love.	X	
4. The Church is for couples spacing the number of children using Natural Fertility Awareness.	X	
5. The Church allows couples to use Natural Fertility Awareness to permanently avoid pregnancy.		X
6. The Church is against IVF because children conceived in a test tube are not really human.		X
7. The Church is against IVF because she doesn't want the marriage bed to be replaced by the laboratory.	X	
8. The Church is against IVF because she doesn't care about the suffering of infertile couples.		X

Natural Fertility Awareness is a method of working out the natural periods of fertility and infertility that are present in every woman's monthly cycle. This is not to be confused with older, less reliable methods such as the Rhythm Method, but is based on observations of natural changes to the woman's body.

[1] This activity is based on Dr C O'Donnell's *Questions & Answers on Sex and Marriage.*

God created human beings to be a union of body and soul. The fact that human beings are created as a union of body and soul means the body is never 'something' but always 'someone' who shares in the dignity of the 'image of God'.

One of the reasons why God made us a union of body and soul is so we could form loving relationships with each other, create children to love, and could be capable of knowing and loving him.

We can see signs of God's design and purpose in nature.

The Church teaches that we can come to know God in two ways:

- through our reason observing nature and ourselves, and
- through God's Word in the Bible and the life of the Church.

The signs of purpose and order in the universe are positive indications that God is the origin and end of everything. The Church doesn't accept extreme theories of evolution that believe that human beings are the random products of chance and accidents. Instead, it holds that there is a purpose and direction to evolution, which is the emergence of self-conscious beings capable of reason and love.

God created masculinity and femininity to reveal our spiritual nature and share in his creation of new life. The Church teaches that sexual love expresses in a profound way our nature as beings created to be a union of body and soul, made in the image of God. The 'body language' of sexual love in marriage says, 'You're the most important person in my life'; 'I love you so much I give you my body'. 'I love every aspect of you so much that I want to have a child with you, who will be part of both of us'.

Jesus reveals and heals our capacity for self-giving love. The Church teaches that we can only know our true dignity and the depth of our ability to love through Jesus Christ. Jesus Christ in his perfect love shows us what it means to be fully human.

Are you ready to accept children lovingly from God?

As a couple take a few minutes to discuss the following questions: (say 5 mins)

- What do we mean when we say that children are a gift from God?
- Would you want your children to be brought up in the Catholic faith? Why?

- The Church understands that 'new life is not the result of each and every act of sexual intercourse' due to the woman's God-given, natural cycle of monthly fertility and infertility. Furthermore, the Church also teaches that were there are 'well-grounded reasons for spacing births, arising from the physical or psychological condition of husband or wife, or from external circumstances' (Pope Paul VI, *Humanae Vitae*), married couples may then take advantage of Natural Fertility Awareness to abstain from sexual relations during the woman's fertile period, and have sexual intercourse during the infertile period. This does not go against God's will for our fertility because the couple are using the natural, God-given cycles for their correct purpose.
- God, in his wisdom, has given us a natural, simple way of being responsible parents that involves our intelligence, self-control and loving consideration. However, the couple must ensure that their motivation is the good of the family and not some selfish desire.

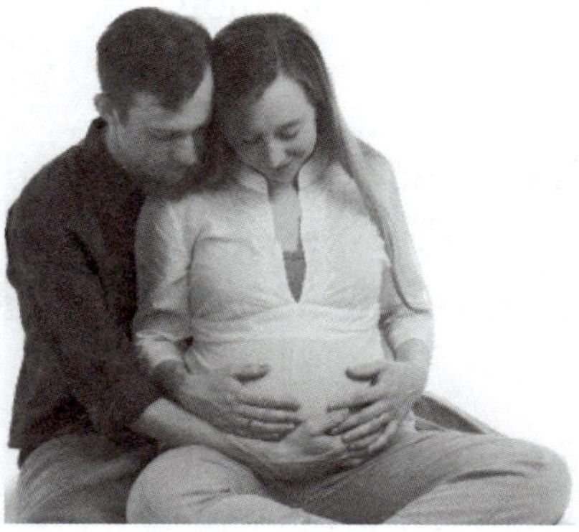

> A child does not come from outside as something added on to the mutual love of the spouses, but springs from the very heart of that mutual giving, as its fruit and fulfilment... called to give life, spouses share in the creative power and fatherhood of God... they are co-operating with the love of God the Creator.
>
> (*CCC* 2366-7)

However, the Church is against both contraception and IVF as they artificially break the inseparable bond between the act of sexual love and openness to fertility. In addition, contraception also makes the act of love a 'lie' by withholding one of the essential qualities of marriage: openness to fertility. The most important and special message that the body language between wife and husband communicates is, "I love every aspect of you so much" – it does not add "except for your fertility".

Action Planning

As a couple consider what you will do as a result of this session. You might like to consider the following:

- Discuss together God's meaning and purpose for sexual love and your approach to having children.
- Find out about Natural Fertility Awareness. Practitioner teachers of the 'ovulation method' or 'multiple-indicators' can be found on the web.

Session 5 Jesus' helping hand

AIM

To see how a proper understanding of who Jesus is helps us understand what happens when we receive the Sacrament of Marriage. To appreciate the importance of this sacrament in helping us face the difficult times in our marriage

OBJECTIVES

By the end of this session, you will be able to:

- Explain what a sacrament is and how sacraments help and support us through life
- Highlight why marriage is a sacrament
- Indicate your approaches to dealing with change and suffering
- Apply some practical actions to help with change and suffering

"If Christ has not been raised, then our preaching is in vain and your faith is in vain." (I Corinthians 15:14)

- During the marriage service, what do you think happens when you make your vows to each other before the priest or deacon, and in front of your family and friends?
- To whom are you making your promises to form a close, personal, permanent, faithful and fruitful union?

Symbols and Sacraments

Symbols are more than just things, they communicate and make real the person we love; they represent the other person and cause us to remember them or something about them.

Sacraments are symbols arising from the life, death and resurrection of Jesus. Jesus took ordinary, everyday things, such as water, oil, bread, wine, and certain words, and gave them a special meaning and power, that make him really and truly present. In the sacraments we receive 'grace', which also means 'gift'. However, it's not the gift of an object or thing, it's the gift of God's love which, if we accept it and believe in it, can empower and transform us.

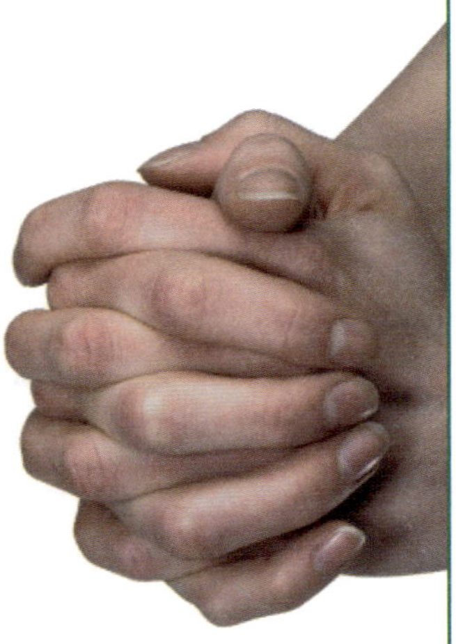

Whoever goes to the Lord for safety, whoever remains under the protection of the Almighty, can say to him, "You are my defender and protector. You are my God: in you I trust"... God says, "I will save those who love me and will protect those who acknowledge me as Lord. When they call to me, I will answer them; when they are in trouble, I will be with them."

(Psalm 91:1, 2, 14, 15)

Who do you say Jesus is?

Read the following passages and decide which one most closely expresses your beliefs. (Take 5 mins).

Version One: Jesus pretended that he was God, and knowingly misled people by claiming to forgive people's sins, heal people of all kinds of disease and by challenging the corruption and exploitation done in the name of God.

Jesus was arrested and put on trial by the Jewish religious authorities for claiming to be God. Facing the death penalty, Jesus maintained his fraud before a hostile court and a sympathetic Roman politician who bent over backwards to let him go. Jesus was tortured and publically disgraced, and finally killed by means of the most feared method of execution, crucifixion.

Once he was dead, and buried, his followers pretended that he had physically come back to life, and immediately made converts from among the people who had personally witnessed his public exposure as a fraud and his shameful death.

Version Two: Jesus was insane and suffered from the delusion that he was God, and created mass hysteria by claiming to forgive people's sins, heal people of all kinds of disease and by challenging the corruption and exploitation done in the name of God. In a highly sophisticated religious culture based on detailed knowledge of Scripture and public debate, despite being mad, Jesus gained a reputation as a convincing and moving orator and debater, who defeated all attempts to trap him into breaking religious and political laws.

Jesus was arrested and put on trial by the Jewish religious authorities for claiming to be God. Facing the death penalty, Jesus maintained a dignified silence under intense pressure from a hostile court and a sympathetic Roman politician who bent over backwards to let him go. Jesus was tortured and publically disgraced, and finally killed by means of the most feared method of execution, crucifixion. During the whole harrowing ordeal Jesus retained his composure and was rational to his dying breath.

Once he was dead, and buried, his followers completely deluded themselves that he had physically come back to life, even to the point of them being tortured and killed for believing Jesus was God. They immediately made converts from among the people who had personally witnessed his public exposure as a mad man and his shameful death.

Version three: Jesus knew he was the Son of God and had been aware since his birth as a human being of his relationship with God the Father and God the Holy Spirit. Faced with the full range of human suffering, Jesus forgave sins, healed people of diseases, and challenged the corruption and exploitation done in the name of God.

Jesus knew that his conflict with the forces of evil would lead to his arrest, torture and execution on the Cross, but he accepted that this was the price that he was uniquely called to pay to free us from our addiction to sin, to mend the estrangement in our relationship with God, and to show us that God loved us so much that, though he was sinless, he was willing to die for us, sinners. Jesus was arrested and put on trial by the Jewish religious authorities for claiming to be God. Facing the death penalty, Jesus publically claimed to be the Son of God, and maintained a dignified silence before a Roman politician who bent over backwards to let him go.

Three days later, despite precautions taken by the Jewish and Roman authorities, Jesus rose from the dead, confirming his claim to be God. Though at first the apostles didn't believe that Jesus had been resurrected, they couldn't deny what they saw with their own eyes, and what they could touch with their own hands. Given authority and power by Jesus, the apostles immediately made converts from among the people who had personally witnessed his public trial, execution and shameful death, and saw the visible effect of Jesus' resurrection on his followers.

"Everyone who reads the Gospels with an open mind agrees that Jesus was a good and wise man, a great and profound teacher. Most non-religious people, and even many people of other religions, like Gandhi, see him as history's greatest moral teacher. He is, in short, eminently trustworthy...

More than any other man in history, Jesus had the three essential virtues every human being needs and wants: wisdom, love and creativity. He wisely and cannily saw into people's hearts, behind their words. He solved insolvable problems. He also gave totally to others, including his very life... The most common reaction of those who met Jesus was 'wonder'... Jesus was the most wonderful person in history." (cf. Peter Kreeft & Ronald Tacelli, *Handbook of Christian Apologetics*, p.155,159).

The Sacrament of Marriage

There are two main reasons why we need the sacrament to be married. Firstly, we need it on a personal level to help us keep the promises we make to each other – to really live a marriage of love for each other. Secondly, we need the sacrament of marriage on a social level so that we can make God's love present in this world.

The Church holds the exchange of consent between the spouses to be the indispensable element that "makes the marriage." If consent is lacking there is no marriage. The consent consists in a "human act by which the partners mutually give themselves to each other": "I take you to be my wife" - "I take you to be my husband." This consent, that binds the spouses to each other, finds its fulfilment in the two "becoming one flesh". (CCC 1626-1627)

Dealing with change

- **Step 1** Agree on one or two major changes you foresee affecting your marriage (perhaps having children, moving house or moving to a different part of the country).
- **Step 2** Take a few minutes to think individually about them. What are the positive things you think will come out of that change? What are the negatives or downsides?
- **Step 3** When you have done that compare notes with each other. Are your views the same or different and how?
- Spend a few minutes sharing the results with the group.

However you deal with change, and in particular suffering, there are a few important pointers to always remember, all of which are strengthened through the grace we receive through the sacrament of marriage.

- **Communicate:** Remember the importance of effective listening and speaking. Do not cut yourself off from one another but be sensitive to one another's need for 'space'. Be honest with one another.
- **Practise the virtues:** Especially kindness, be particularly attentive and loving to each other. Be prepared to persevere, to hold on when the going gets tough rather than cut and run.
- **Pray:** We will be talking more about this in the next session.
- **Use your community network:** During times of change and suffering it is important to remember that as a couple you are not on your own, but part of a larger net work of care and love, either through your family, friends or parish. Sometimes it may be necessary to seek outside help to cope with overwhelming problems, such as grief or depression.
- **Humour:** It can help us to laugh at our predicaments, which may make it possible to transcend anxiety and pain. However, this only works if the other factors in this list are in place, or it can become another disguise for anger at the other person's expense, and / or hurtful and destructive.

If you live your marriage with awareness and acceptance of the meaning and purpose given it by God then your lives will be enriched and strengthened by the gift – the grace – of the sacrament of marriage.

Christ dwells with them, gives them the strength to take up their crosses and so follow him, to rise again after they have fallen, to forgive one another, to bear one another's burdens, to "be subject to one another out of reverence for Christ", and to love one another with supernatural, tender, and fruitful love.

(CCC 1642)

Action Planning

As a couple consider what you will do as a result of this session. You might like to consider the following:

- Discuss together what helps or hinders you when you are dealing with change.
- Share together some of the things which have already caused suffering in your life.

Session 6 Loving each other in Christ

AIM

To appreciate the significance and meaning of the different parts of the wedding service and that marriage is made in prayer

OBJECTIVES

By the end of this session, you will be able to:

- Explain who confers the sacrament of marriage on the couple, before the Church and sealed by God
- State the significance of the different elements of the marriage liturgy
- Explain the meaning of the symbols of marriage
- Prepare for your own marriage service
- Describe the importance of prayer

Promises before God and his Church

As bride and groom during the wedding service you will both make promises to live according to the purpose and meaning God has given marriage. In this activity 'match' the promises from the wedding service with one of the four essential qualities of marriage: personal union, indissolubility, faithfulness and openness to life.

Promises from Marriage Rite	Essential quality of Marriage
Are you ready freely and without reservation to give yourselves to each other in marriage? Bridegroom: **I am**. Bride: **I am**.	
Are you ready to love and honour each other as man and wife for the rest of your lives? Bridegroom: **I am**. Bride: **I am**.	
Are you ready to accept children lovingly from God, and bring them up according to the law of Christ and his Church? Bridegroom: **I am**. Bride: **I am**.	
Bridegroom and Bride: I call upon these persons here present to witness that I, NN do take thee, NN to be my lawful wedded wife (husband), to have and to hold from this day forward, for better for worse, for richer for poorer, in sickness and in health, to love and to cherish till death us do part.	

Consent

The priest or deacon invites the couple to declare their consent:

Priest or Deacon: Since it is your intention to enter marriage, declare your consent before God and his Church.

(*To the Bridegroom*) N.N., will you take N.N. here present for your lawful wife, according to the rite of our holy Mother the Church? *Bridegroom*: **I will.**

(*To the Bride*) N.N., will you take N.N. here present for your lawful husband, according to the rite of our holy Mother the Church? *Bride*: **I will.**

The Bride and Bridegroom join their right hands.The Bridegroom then says after the Priest or Deacon, or reads:

Bridegroom: I call upon these persons here present to witness that I, N.N. (full name, including surname), do take thee, N.N. (full name, including surname), to be my lawful wedded wife to have and to hold from this day forward, for better for worse, for richer for poorer, in sickness and in health, to love and to cherish, till death do us part.

They separate their hands for a moment and then rejoin them. Then the Bride says after the Priest or Deacon, or reads:

Bride: I call upon these persons here present to witness that I, N.N. (full name, including surname), do take thee, N.N. (full name, including surname), to be my lawful wedded husband to have and to hold from this day forward, for better for worse, for richer for poorer, in sickness and in health, to love and to cherish, till death do us part.

At this moment you have both conferred on each other the sacrament of marriage, and you are now married. The Priest or Deacon then receives your consent on behalf of the Church with this prayer:

Priest or Deacon: You have declared your consent before the Church. May the Lord in his goodness strengthen your consent and fill you both with his blessings. What God had joined together, let no man put asunder.

Marriage bond: The blessing and exchange of rings is a symbol of the couple's consent and creation of their marriage bond blessed by God. When you consummate your marriage through sexual intercourse you definitively express the meaning and purpose of the vows and consent you made during the rite of marriage – total self-giving love to the point where two become one.

Visit to the church

The church is a sacred place where we have the privilege of sharing in God's life and where we share our lives with God. A 'sacred space' means it's been set aside for the worship of God and for our reception of his sacraments. It is not like any other public space, such as a public hall, cinema or theatre. Everything here, the art, the architecture, the objects, communicates one thing – this is a sacred place where God is present. You belong here, this is your church. You have as much right to be here as the priest, deacon, or anyone else. The one thing that is required from us all is respect. (That's why, for example, wedding guests are asked to switch off their mobile phones and be very discreet about taking photographs).

- **Sanctuary light** The red candle on the sanctuary is lit permanently to remind us that Jesus is present in the Tabernacle, which is the most holy place in the whole church.
- **Sign of the cross** As a sign of respect, we cross ourselves when we enter the Church. It reminds us of Jesus' totally self-giving love in dying on the cross; it reminds us that we are called to show the same love to each other.
- **Genuflection** This is made by touching the ground with one's right or left knee. Catholics genuflect before entering the bench where they will sit, or going to read from the lectern or to act as an Extraordinary Minister of Holy Communion, as a sign of reverence before the presence of the Blessed Sacrament in the Tabernacle or on the altar.

> On entering a church or in passing before the altar, kneel down all the way without haste or hurry, putting your heart into what you do, and let your whole attitude say, Thou art the great God.
>
> (*Romano Guardini*)

- **Kneeling** It is usual for people to kneel, if they are not disabled, when they first enter their bench as a sign of respect to the presence of Jesus. Kneeling is a sacred sign that shows our recognition of God's power and holiness. When you receive the Nuptial Blessing at the conclusion of the marriage rite you will both be asked to kneel, which expresses your recognition of God's power and purpose for your lives together as husband and wife.
- **Standing** Like making the sign of the cross and kneeling standing has a special meaning in the Church. Standing means we are attentive to God, ready for action according to

his will. We stand when the Gospel is proclaimed by the priest or deacon, we stand when, as godparents at a baptism, we make our proclamation of faith. As a bride and bridegroom you will stand when you make your promises to be faithful to your marriage vows and consent to be married before the altar.

- **Candles** Light is one of the essentials of life, and Jesus described himself as 'the light of the world' (John 8:12). A candle is a very simple object, but it has an inherent power and beauty that communicates in a church that this is a holy, sacred place, a place where we share in the life of God, and we share our lives with God and each other.
- **The Altar** This is one of the most important parts of a church and is often situated on a raised or separate area called the Sanctuary, meaning 'holy place'. It is here that the sacrament of sacraments is celebrated, the sacrifice of the Mass, the consecration of the bread and wine that become the Body and Blood of Jesus, the real and true presence of God. The altar is also the table of the Lord to which all people are invited, as one family around the family table. (cf. *CCC* 1182).
- **The Tabernacle** As we mentioned earlier, this is also deeply holy, because the Lord is really present in the Blessed Sacrament of the Altar, the Body of Jesus. (cf. *CCC* 1183).
- **The Lectern** This is another prominent feature of the church, from which the Word of God contained in the Bible, is proclaimed to the people. As well as being present in the sacraments, we believe that God is present in the living word proclaimed in the church. (cf. *CCC* 1184). As part of your preparation for your marriage you'll be asked to choose passages from the Bible to be read during the rite of marriage.

- **Baptismal font** In the font people receive the fundamental sacrament of Christian life, baptism, which frees them from Original Sin and joins them, 'grafts them', into the life and graces of Jesus. Hopefully, in due time this is where you will bring your children to become members of God's family. (cf. *CCC* 1185).
- **Confessionals** The sacrament of reconciliation, involving confession, absolution and penance, is related to Baptism, and is another sacrament of healing and life-giving grace. In these confessionals Catholics receive Jesus' forgiveness for their sins, and spiritual advice and encouragement. A very good way of preparing for your wedding day is to go to confession to make a fresh start, which we all need to do from time to time.

Marriages are made in prayer

> *'Marriages are made in prayer', which explains the most important thing you need to do to have a wonderful wedding day – pray!*

The rite of marriage is a sequence of prayers and promises, which are best understood and said by the bride and bridegroom in a spirit of prayer.

Prayer can be formal and the Church has a rich heritage of prayers for every occasion including your marriage. However, you will really feel the wonder of prayer if you can also say informal or private prayers. As with many things that you want to accomplish in your day it can help to build in a routine: having special times for prayer even if it is only a few minutes (e.g., morning offering, night time prayers, grace at meals). Don't leave it till you are too tired to give it your best effort though, try to pray at the best part of the day. But that doesn't mean that prayers cannot be said at any time.

A nice way to structure informal prayers is this three step method: TSP.

- **T** – Thanks. Thank God for the good things that have happened today or in your life.
- **S** – Sorry. Say sorry for the bad things that have happened today or in your life.
- **P** – Please. Ask God for help for things or people that you care about.

Nuptial Blessing

Father, by your power you have made everything out of nothing. In the beginning you created the universe and made mankind in your own likeness. You gave man the constant help of women so that man and woman should no longer be two, but one flesh, and you teach us that what you have united may never be divided.

Father, you have made the union of man and woman so holy a mystery that it symbolizes the marriage of Christ and his Church.

Look with love upon this woman, your daughter, who is to be joined to her husband in marriage. She asks your blessing. Give her the grace of love and peace. May she always follow the example of the holy women whose praises are sung in the scriptures.

May her husband put his trust in her and recognize that she is his equal and heir with him to the life of grace. May he always honour her and love her as Christ loves his bride, the Church.

Father, keep them always true to your commandments. Keep them faithful in marriage and let them be living examples of Christian life. Give them the strength which comes from the gospel so that they may be witnesses of Christ to others.

Bless them with children and help them to be good parents. May they live to see their children's children. And, after a happy old age, grant them fullness of life with the saints in the kingdom of heaven.

We ask this through Christ our Lord.

Amen.